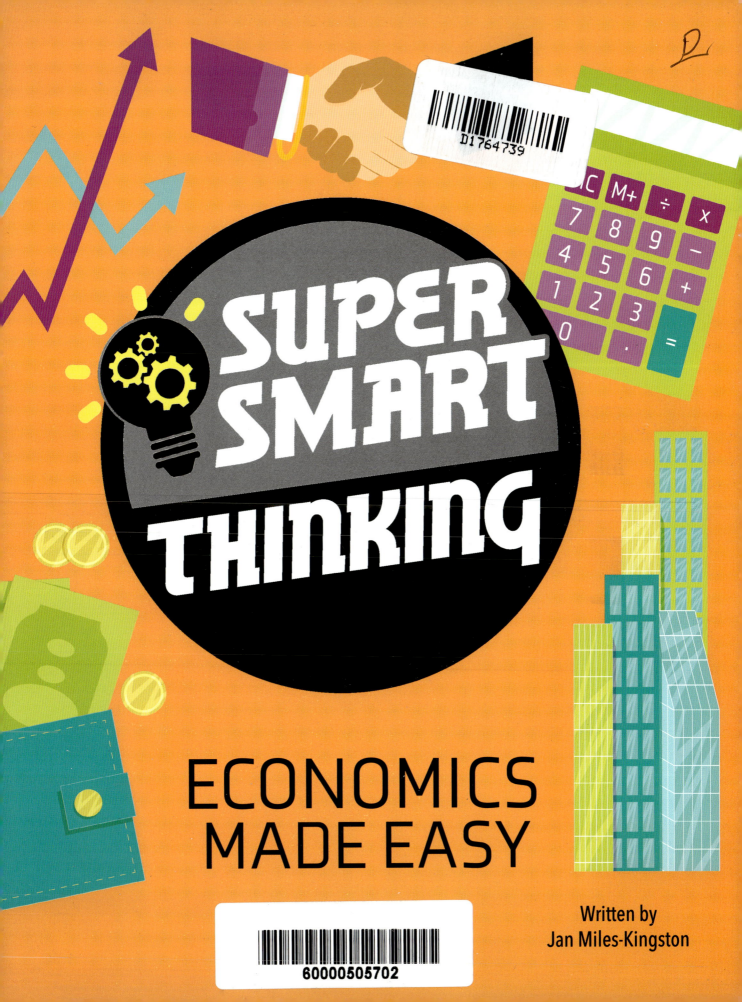

SUPER SMART THINKING

ECONOMICS MADE EASY

Written by
Jan Miles-Kingston

First published in Great Britain in 2021
by Wayland

Copyright © Hodder and Stoughton, 2021

Editor: John Hort
Design and illustration: Collaborate Ltd

HB ISBN: 978 1 5263 1720 9
PB ISBN: 978 1 5263 1721 6

Printed and bound in Dubai

MIX
Paper from
responsible sources
FSC® C104740

FSC
www.fsc.org

Wayland, an imprint of
Hachette Children's Group
Part of Hodder and Stoughton
Carmelite House
50 Victoria Embankment
London EC4Y 0DZ
An Hachette UK Company

www.hachette.co.uk
www.hachettechildrens.co.uk

CONTENTS

WHAT IS ECONOMICS? 4

THINKING LIKE AN ECONOMIST 6

HOW DO PEOPLE DECIDE WHAT TO BUY? 8

HOW DO FIRMS DECIDE WHAT TO SELL? 10

HOW DO MARKETS WORK? 12

WAYS THAT MARKETS FAIL 14

SMALL WAYS GOVERNMENTS TRY TO HELP 16

THE BIG PICTURE FOR A WHOLE ECONOMY 18

IMPORTANT AIMS FOR GOVERNMENTS 20

BIG WAYS GOVERNMENTS TRY TO HELP 22

WHY SHOULD COUNTRIES WORK TOGETHER? 24

GLOBALISATION 26

CHALLENGES FOR THE FUTURE.......................... 28

GLOSSARY 30

FURTHER INFORMATION 31

INDEX 32

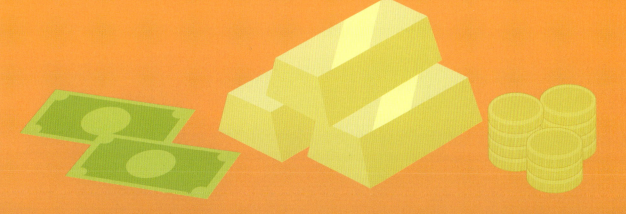

WHAT IS ECONOMICS?

Welcome to economics! This subject looks at how to meet people's needs and wants using available **resources**. It can help you make decisions, whether as an individual, a businessperson or a world leader!

THE ECONOMIC PROBLEM

The economic problem links all economics: if there are limited resources available, how can this be balanced with unlimited wants for things? It is an impossible problem to solve completely! Thinking about it can help us to make better decisions about how to use the world's scarce resources.

The scarcity of resources means people must make decisions about what they want most. Economists look at how people prioritise their choices and what they decide to sacrifice. This insight into how people think can help economists predict how they will act in the future.

The economic problem can be summarised and divided like this:

ECONOMIC PROBLEM

UNLIMITED WANTS + LIMITED RESOURCES

1 WHAT TO PRODUCE?

2 HOW TO PRODUCE?

3 WHO BENEFITS?

There are lots of different answers to these questions …

THINKING LIKE AN ECONOMIST

Economists learn to think in a way that is both **logical** and creative. They look at lots of different economic actions and reason what might happen. It is like following the tumbling path of a line of dominoes.

CHAINS OF REASONING

Economic chains of reasoning connect causes to effects, link by link.

This reasoning technique helps economists predict futures. They work out how likely different effects are and put a price on their costs or benefits. Economic actions where benefits are greater than costs are good for **society** and a good use of resources. This is **cost-benefit analysis**.

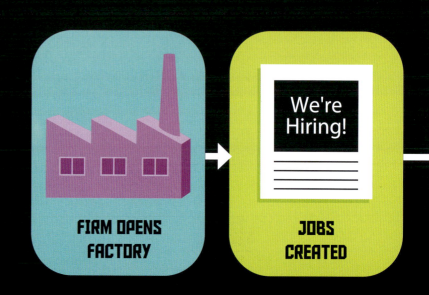

FIRM OPENS FACTORY

We're Hiring!

JOBS CREATED

MODELS

Reasoning in economics takes a scientific approach by using **models**. A model builds up a simplified economic scenario and changes one thing at a time to try to foresee possible consequences. For example, the sales of a particular chocolate bar and the impact of a change in its price. This could then be used to forecast sales at different prices.

When using models, there are key economic agents to think about:

Consumers
Who are the buyers and users of products.

Suppliers
Who are the producers and sellers of products.

Government
Who are a group of people who run the country and manage its **economy**.

SELF-INTEREST

Models simplify the real world by making assumptions. In economics, it is assumed that consumers and producers are motivated by **self-interest**. This makes it possible to argue how consumers and producers are likely to act in different situations.

As well as developing reasoning skills, economists use mathematical skills and become expert at interpreting data, whether it be in tables, graphs or any form whatsoever!

PEOPLE MOVE TO THE AREA

MORE COMPETITION TO BUY HOUSES

SOLD!

INCREASE IN HOUSE PRICES

This is an example of a chain of reasoning.

HOW DO PEOPLE DECIDE WHAT TO BUY?

In economics, consumers' economic decisions are motivated by maximising their satisfaction. The human brain is an incredible computer and is constantly working in the background to calculate satisfaction from products, instantly valuing and converting them into a reasonable price.

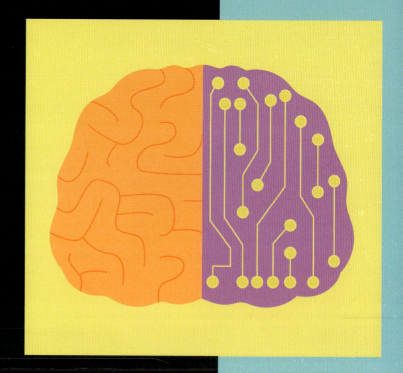

THE LAW OF DEMAND

… is built on this idea of self-interest. If the price of a product increases, some consumers will decide that the price is not worth the satisfaction they receive from it, so they will stop buying it.

Do you think self-interest is the key motivator for your decision to buy products?

Economists use diagrams to reason, predict and argue. The law of **demand** can be shown on a diagram that plots price changes with the resulting changes in quantity demanded. Demand from individual consumers can be added together to give the picture for a whole economy.

Would you have demanded fewer apples if the price increased as shown in the diagram?

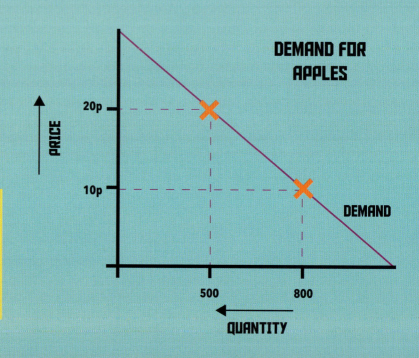

DEMAND FOR APPLES

The price of a product is the most important factor when buying products, but non-price factors also affect demand:

Population
Changes in population affect the level of demand. For example, if the population has a **baby boom** there will be a surge in demand for nappies.

Income
Changes in the amount of money earnt affects what individuals can afford to buy.

Taste
Changing fashions can affect demand. For example, influencers on social media can help increase demand for a product.

Substitutes
Changes to rival products, such as their prices, will have an impact on demand for competing products.

BEHAVIOURAL ECONOMICS

… looks further into the **psychology** behind economic decisions. An example is impulse buying where consumers make a sudden decision to buy a product without fully thinking through its value. This psychology is used by businesses and **governments** to nudge individuals towards specific decisions. Be aware!

Shops often place tempting items like chocolate or chewing gum close to the checkouts, in the hope customers will buy them on impulse when purchasing other things.

HOW DO FIRMS DECIDE WHAT TO SELL?

Firms are suppliers that are the sellers and producers of products. Their main motivation is to make profit. Profit is the money left over after all the costs of production are subtracted from the money that consumers have paid for the products.

THE LAW OF SUPPLY

Economists use diagrams to predict the likely behaviour of firms. In this case, if the price of a product rises in a **market**, this is a signal to firms that consumers are competing with each other to buy their product, which pushes the price up. This higher price means that there is a good chance of more profit for firms, so firms will be motivated to **supply** as many more products as possible. This is the law of supply: when the price rises, the quantity supplied increases too.

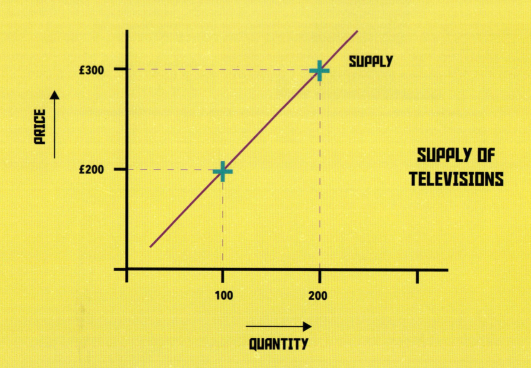

FIRMS' OBJECTIVES

Firms also track their costs of production, such as wages and **raw materials**, to work out their profit and decide whether to supply.

Firms may have different reasons for selling products. For example, **fair trade** is where firms choose not to maximise their profits, because they buy products from suppliers in less developed countries at a 'fair' price. This 'fair' price is higher than the price they could pay some suppliers. These 'fair' prices enable the suppliers to improve life in their communities, such as paying their workers more to enable a better **standard of living**.

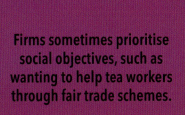

Firms sometimes prioritise social objectives, such as wanting to help tea workers through fair trade schemes.

HOW DO MARKETS WORK?

Microeconomics studies demand and supply at a small level, such as for individual product markets.

MARKET FORCES

A market is where products are bought and sold. It can be a physical place but, often, it exists in virtual reality. There are an infinite number of markets working in the world all the time – consumers and suppliers making lots of economic decisions that, driven by self-interest, come together to ensure different products are made and sold.

Think how many different decisions will have been made by different consumers and suppliers at different stages of production to make this book. It is as if there are invisible forces at work!

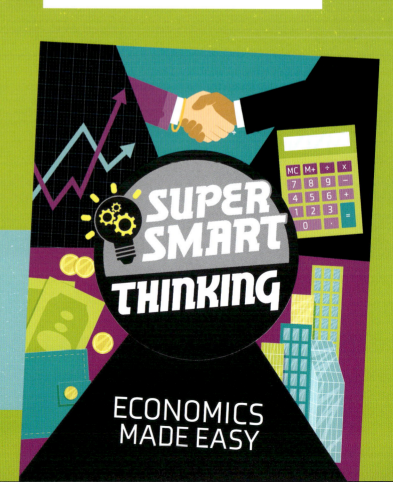

SUPER SMART THINKING

ECONOMICS MADE EASY

DEMAND AND SUPPLY

The decisions to buy and sell a specific product can be shown using a demand and supply diagram. This diagram shows the demand and supply of books.

Consumers buy books up to where the price paid is equal to the satisfaction that they expect from the book, so where the price offered by suppliers equals a price on the demand curve. Suppliers will be motivated to supply more if there is more profit, so they will keep supplying until they reach the top price where consumers are willing to buy all the books made. The market settles at the point where demand matches supply.

SUPPLY AND DEMAND OF BOOKS

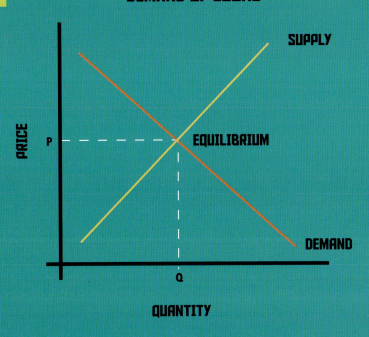

EQUILIBRIUM

… is the word used for where demand equals supply in a market. When markets find the right equilibrium, it has helped reduce the economic problem. Consumers and suppliers have thought about their fixed resources and made choices about what to buy and sell to maximise their self-interest.

For example, resources that become scarcer are rationed as their price increases and demand falls in response. This is the market system at work!

Diamonds are an example of a scarce resource, which is why they have such a high value.

13

WAYS THAT MARKETS FAIL

The market system is not perfect. It can fail to **allocate** scarce resources to the best uses for society. In fact, markets sometimes worsen the economic problem.

IMPERFECT INFORMATION

Information is vital in the market system, so consumers and producers can make the right economic decisions. For example, when a consumer buys a burger, they may not make a fully informed economic decision if they do not know what the ingredients are or how they could impact their health. This may mean demand for burgers is too high in the market system. This would mean too many scarce resources would be put into the production of burgers.

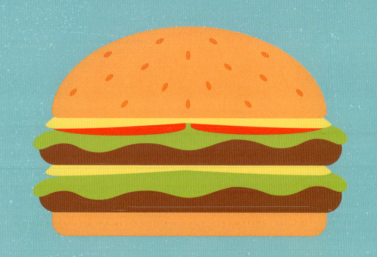

Consumers often face an information gap when deciding whether to buy products. For example, when buying a second-hand car, it is likely that the car dealer will have better technical knowledge about the condition of their cars. If one of the economic agents has more information than another, it can lead to wrong choices being made.

Consumers may be more likely to suffer from imperfect information, but suppliers can also be affected. For example, insurance companies may suffer from imperfect information when they agree to insure a new driver.

MARKETS AND SELF-INTEREST

The market system is built upon decisions based on self-interest. This means that individual consumers and suppliers do not look at the impact of their economic decisions on the rest of society. These impacts are called externalities. For example, in the fashion industry, clothes production may have a cost for individuals who are not consuming or producing the clothes, such as harm from pollution due to chemicals used. These costs are outside of suppliers' costs of production, so are not included when working out profit, leading to supply being too high.

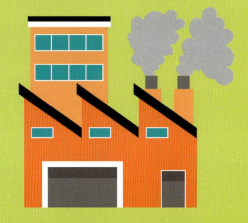

There may also be benefits that are not included in the market system. For example, consumers may not fully realise the advantages of buying healthy food beyond their own personal benefit.

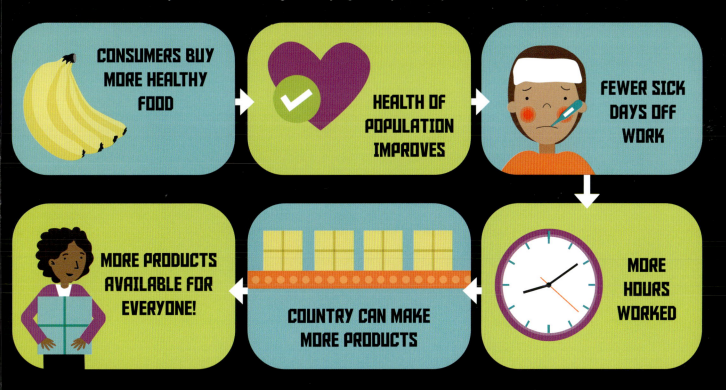

CONSUMERS BUY MORE HEALTHY FOOD

HEALTH OF POPULATION IMPROVES

FEWER SICK DAYS OFF WORK

MORE HOURS WORKED

COUNTRY CAN MAKE MORE PRODUCTS

MORE PRODUCTS AVAILABLE FOR EVERYONE!

At the point of deciding whether to buy the healthy food, not many consumers would go through this thought process, so their demand is unlikely to be high enough in the market system.

A TRUE BALANCE

Economists adjust demand and supply so that these hidden costs and benefits are included. This gives an equilibrium that reflects the best use of resources from society's viewpoint.

SMALL WAYS GOVERNMENTS TRY TO HELP

Many countries allow the market system to work freely for many products. However, governments may intervene to reduce any failure of the market to include all the costs and benefits of a product and to allocate resources to products that are better for society.

GOVERNMENT INTERVENTION

A government may use the market system by changing the price of a product.

Government tax

For example, many governments add **tax** to products that are seen as harmful, such as sugary drinks. Tax is money that is paid to the government. It can be taken as a proportion of an individual's earnings or a firm's profits. In this example it is added to the price of a product. It is hoped that consumers follow the law of demand so as the price rises, it should make the quantity demanded fall.

Government subsidies

A government may think that a product should be consumed more for the benefit of society, such as rail services. More people using rail services means fewer people in cars, which decreases pollution. The government gives money to firms, known as a **subsidy**, so they can lower prices, so people demand more.

Government provision

In some cases, a government may think a particular product or service is so important for society that it provides it directly to consumers themselves, such as health services and education.

GOVERNMENT FAILURE

Sometimes government intervention has little impact and costs a country more than it benefits it. Intervention can also create more problems. For example, governments around the world encouraged farmers to grow crops for fuel to try to reduce the pollution from using fossil fuels. They subsidised farmers to switch to growing **biofuels**, but an unanticipated consequence was that food prices went up. Sometimes government intervention in markets may fail to help reduce the economic problem.

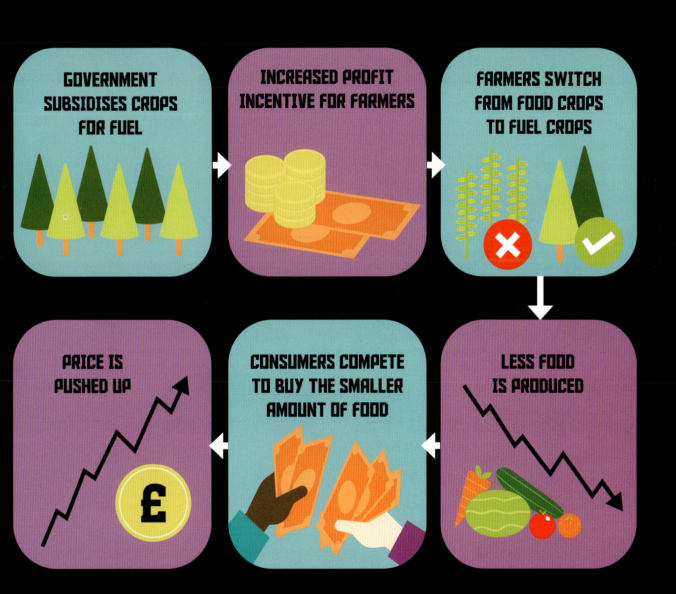

GOVERNMENT SUBSIDISES CROPS FOR FUEL

INCREASED PROFIT INCENTIVE FOR FARMERS

FARMERS SWITCH FROM FOOD CROPS TO FUEL CROPS

PRICE IS PUSHED UP

CONSUMERS COMPETE TO BUY THE SMALLER AMOUNT OF FOOD

LESS FOOD IS PRODUCED

What might be a consequence of the increased price of food?

THE BIG PICTURE FOR A WHOLE ECONOMY

Macroeconomics is the study of the big picture for a whole economy. It adds together all the individual markets to form total demand and supply for all products and services in a country.

TOTAL DEMAND AND SUPPLY

Total demand in an economy comes from spending by consumers, government and firms. Factors that influence these groups and their decision to buy include changes in income, uncertainty about the future and how much the government decides to intervene.

Total supply in an economy is the total amount of products and services that suppliers are willing to supply at different price levels. This is influenced by changes in costs of production, the impact of government intervention and changes in the quality or quantity of resources available, such as an increase in the skills of workers.

GROSS DOMESTIC PRODUCT

The equilibrium of total demand and total supply shows the total amount of products and services that are made in a country. This total output is known as **gross domestic product** (GDP). Economists follow changes in this over time to predict how much a country may make in the future.

MARKET VS. COMMAND

Different governments take different approaches to their economy. A market economy is where there is little government intervention and the market system decides how resources are allocated. A command economy is where the government plans how resources are allocated and controls economic decisions. Many countries now have mixed economies, where some economic decisions are left to the market system and others are taken by the government.

COMMAND ECONOMY ⟷ MIXED ECONOMY ⟷ MARKET ECONOMY

All types of economy aim to reduce the economic problem and do the best for society, but they use different ways to try to achieve these aims.

IMPORTANT AIMS FOR GOVERNMENTS

Most governments have important aims for what they want to achieve in their country's economy. Economists assess how much different actions meet these aims.

PARLIAMENT

ECONOMIC GROWTH

… is often the top priority. It means that an economy increases its output over time. When assessing the success of a government, economic growth and its consequences seem beneficial.

ECONOMIC GROWTH

£

INCREASED OUTPUT NEEDS MORE WORKERS

We're Hiring!

MORE JOBS

HIGHER STANDARD OF LIVING

WORKERS CAN AFFORD MORE PRODUCTS

MORE WORKERS WITH WAGES

UNEMPLOYMENT

Governments aim to have low unemployment. With more workers employed, they can make more products and services, so increase economic growth. Also, with more workers with wages, there may be a better standard of living. The government spends less on unemployment benefits, so can spend more on other areas of the economy or reduce taxes. All of these are positive for society!

INFLATION

Governments try to control **inflation**. Inflation is where prices for products increase over time. If prices increase a lot, it makes it more difficult for a country to sell its products to consumers in other countries as they appear more expensive. This can lead to falling demand for a country's products. It also becomes difficult for consumers and firms to work out if different products are worth their increasing prices, so uncertainty sets in.

PRICES

INCOME INEQUALITY

Another objective for governments is to increase fairness within an economy. One way this is measured is by income inequality. This looks at how incomes are shared between people in a country. If income is shared so that a small number of people receive most of the income, then there is high income inequality.

BIG WAYS GOVERNMENTS TRY TO HELP

As well as trying to help small, specific product markets, governments may try to help the whole economy in a much bigger way. Different macroeconomic policies aim to impact the whole economy.

FISCAL POLICY

… is where the government changes their spending in an economy or the level of taxation. These can impact different aims, such as economic growth and low unemployment.

GOVERNMENT REDUCES INCOME TAX
%

PEOPLE HAVE MORE INCOME LEFT OVER

TOTAL SPENDING IN AN ECONOMY INCREASES

MORE PRODUCTS NEEDED TO MEET THE INCREASED SPENDING
SOLD Out!

INCREASE IN TOTAL OUTPUT

ECONOMIC GROWTH
£

SUPPLY-SIDE POLICY

A government may also use a supply-side policy. These are types of government intervention that increase potential output over time. Examples of these policies include any government measure that makes it easier for firms to supply.

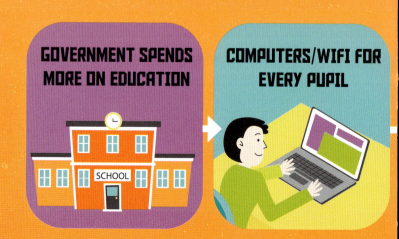

GOVERNMENT SPENDS MORE ON EDUCATION
SCHOOL

COMPUTERS/WIFI FOR EVERY PUPIL

MONETARY POLICY

… involves changing things that affect money in an economy, such as the **interest rate**.
Interest rates are a percentage of money that is added to money saved or loaned by banks.
Some countries have a central bank that controls money to try to impact the economy.
In England this is the Bank of England, and in the USA it is the Federal Reserve.

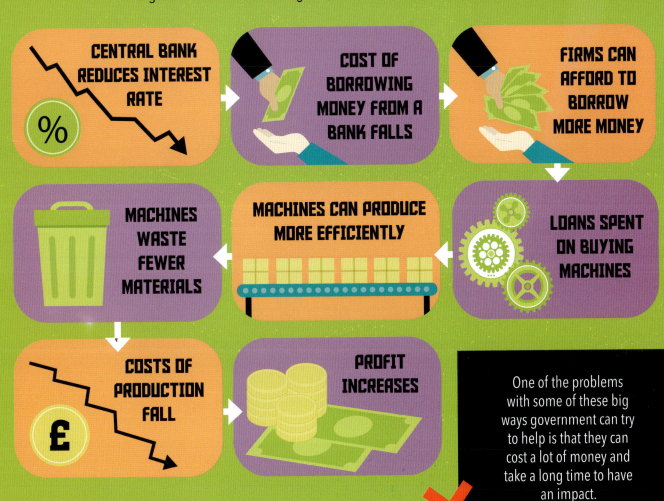

CENTRAL BANK REDUCES INTEREST RATE

COST OF BORROWING MONEY FROM A BANK FALLS

FIRMS CAN AFFORD TO BORROW MORE MONEY

MACHINES WASTE FEWER MATERIALS

MACHINES CAN PRODUCE MORE EFFICIENTLY

LOANS SPENT ON BUYING MACHINES

COSTS OF PRODUCTION FALL

PROFIT INCREASES

One of the problems with some of these big ways government can try to help is that they can cost a lot of money and take a long time to have an impact.

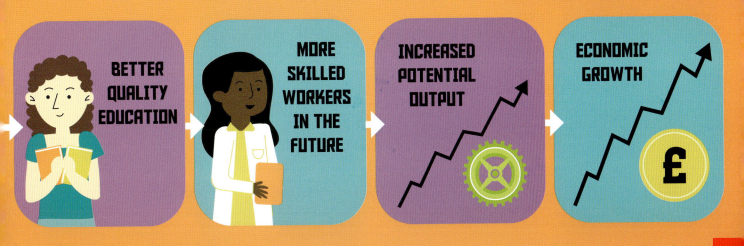

BETTER QUALITY EDUCATION

MORE SKILLED WORKERS IN THE FUTURE

INCREASED POTENTIAL OUTPUT

ECONOMIC GROWTH

WHY SHOULD COUNTRIES WORK TOGETHER?

Countries may work together to help reduce the economic problem. International trade means that countries can export or sell their products to other countries and import or buy products from other countries.

GLOBAL RESOURCES

Different countries have different resources available for production, such as different climates for growing food, different natural resources and workers with different skills. This means some countries are better at making certain products than others. For example, the climate in Britain is less suited to growing bananas than other countries, such as India, so it would take far more resources to try to produce bananas in Britain.

If all countries make their specialist products, as a world we can make more products overall and use fewer scarce resources.

 **SPECIALISATION IN A PRODUCT**

 **REPEATEDLY MAKE THAT PRODUCT**

 **BECOME MORE SKILLED AT PRODUCTION**

 **USE FEWER RESOURCES AND INCREASE OUTPUT**

INTERNATIONAL TRADE

… means that countries can sell some of their specialist products to gain money that can be used to buy specialist products from other countries. This means that individuals in different countries can access a wider range of products, which increases their satisfaction and standard of living.

CLOSED

GLOBAL COMPETITION

If countries work together through trade, this means firms are now competing with other firms across the world. This can motivate firms to work harder to improve the quality of their products and to lower their prices. This is beneficial for consumers, but it may lead to firms that are unable to compete having to close.

GLOBALISATION

Globalisation is when countries around the world become more linked to each other, primarily through international trade.

Globalisation means that almost anything can be made anywhere and sold to anyone. Multinational firms now have factories in some countries, offices in others and shops around the world. For example, there are successful international brands that were originally based in one country but are now made and sold around the world. Can you think of a product that people around the world would recognise?

Improvements in transportation and advances in technology and communications have increased globalisation.

GROWTH OF INTERNET

ENABLED INTERNET BANKING

EASIER TO PAY FOR PRODUCTS IN DIFFERENT COUNTRIES

INCREASED GLOBALISATION

EASIER TO TRADE WORLDWIDE

PROS ...

There are positive consequences of globalisation. It has enabled individuals to buy and firms to sell products worldwide. The increase in competition between firms and increased specialisation has resulted in lower prices and better-quality products. It enables jobs to be created all over the world to supply demand from other countries.

... AND CONS

Globalisation can also lead to challenges. For example, as firms are competing with more firms from around the world, some firms may lose consumers, so have to shut down. This can lead to unemployment and falling standards of living. Governments may help by paying unemployment benefits, encouraging new firms and helping workers find new jobs, but this can cost a lot of money and takes time.

Some multinational firms become so big that they dominate their markets. It makes it hard for other firms to compete and stops other firms joining the market. When a firm becomes the only supplier in the market, it is known as a monopoly. This can be harmful for consumers. For example, because there are now few substitutes, the firm can raise its prices.

PRODUCTION AND PROTECTION

The spending by international firms and the jobs provided can be very important in poorer areas. However, there may need to be rules to help protect the environment and workers to ensure production does not harm the standard of living in a country.

CHALLENGES FOR THE FUTURE

Economists are part of the team trying to solve the challenges of the future. A key focus is on the problem of increasingly scarce resources.

The task for economists is to reduce the economic problem in the present day, as well as looking ahead to how our actions can help it in the future. Actions and decisions made using this idea are **sustainable**. The world can continue with sustainable actions, knowing they should still be possible in the future.

CHANGING HABITS

As the global population grows, there is increased demand for products, which uses up scarce resources. This means there are fewer resources to make products in the future. This returns to the question of how to produce sustainably, for example, by using renewable resources.

POLLUTED PLANET

With increased output, there can also be increased harm for the environment. During production there may be air pollution or discarded plastic packaging may lead to water pollution. These problems can be reduced by changing how products are produced. Research into options that do not harm the environment may help. Economists help predict the costs and benefits of different actions, so that governments, firms and consumers can make decisions on how to reduce pollution.

CLIMATE CHANGE

… will impact the economic problem. Resources may be affected, such as loss of land due to rising sea levels or the impact of changing weather patterns. Economists can look at how economic decisions can respond to and minimise **climate change**.

SAVING THE WORLD

Solving the economic problem both now and for the future is a job for everyone. The world needs economists who are creative problem-solvers, who can look ahead, who are open to all options, who can reason and assess different decisions. It needs people who are alert to problems and mistakes. It needs people who want to make a difference. The world needs YOU!

GLOSSARY

Allocate
To give out, or share, money or other resources

Baby boom
A year or period of time when more babies are born than usual

Biofuel
Fuel made from plants or animals

Climate change
Changes in the Earth's normal weather patterns, especially the increase in the temperature of Earth's atmosphere

Consumer
A person who buys goods or uses services

Cost-benefit analysis
Investigating the relationship between the cost of doing something and the value of the benefit that results from it

Demand
The amount of a product or service that consumers are prepared to buy at different prices

Economy
A system for allocating resources to meet people's needs and wants. This includes the way people spend money and make money in a particular country or area

Fair trade
Organisations and businesses working together so producers are paid a reasonable price for what they have grown or made

Government
The group of people who run the country and manage its economy

Gross domestic product (GDP)
The total amount of products and services that are made in a country over a period of time, usually a year

Incentive
Something that encourages you to do something, such as save energy

Inflation
The rate at which the prices of services and goods increase over time

Interest rate
The percentage rate of money that is charged on a loan or added to savings by banks

Logical
Careful and thoughtful thinking

Market
Any place where buyers and sellers meet to buy and sell products or services

Model
In economics, a model builds up a simplified economic scenario and changes one thing at a time to try to work out all possible consequences

Producer
A person or a business that grows or makes food, goods or materials

Psychology
The scientific study of the mind and how it influences behaviour

Raw material
Any of the natural materials, such as cotton, oil or sugar, before they have been processed for use

Resources
The materials we need and value, such as food, land or diamonds

Self-interest
Only considering your own interests rather than caring about what others need or want

Society
People living together in communities

Standard of living
The daily level of comfort that a person, or a group, experiences, such as access to necessities like food and energy

Subsidy
A sum of money paid by a government to a business to lower the costs of producing certain goods, so that their price can be kept low

Supplier
A producer and seller of a product or products

Supply
The amount of a product or service that businesses are prepared to sell at different prices

Sustainable
Using natural products (such as land or wood) and energy in a way that does not harm the environment

Tax
Money that you pay to the government so that it can pay for public services, such as schools and hospitals

FURTHER INFORMATION

BOOKS

Be A Young Entrepreneur (Wayland, 2016)

Dosh: How to Earn It, Save It, Spend It, Grow It, Give It (Wren and Rook, 2020)

Money Box (series, Franklin Watts, 2019)

WEBSITES

kids.britannica.com/kids/article/economics/353081
A great website that has lots of information on economics and related topics.

www.discovereconomics.co.uk
A website ran by the Royal Economic Society which aims to make economics accessible for children.

INDEX

behavioural economics 9

chains of reasoning 6–7
climate change 29
cost-benefit analysis 6
consumers 7–10, 12–18, 21, 25,
       27–28

economies, different types of 19
externalities 15

fair trade 11
firms 6, 10–11, 16, 18, 21–23, 25–28

globalisation 26–27
governments 7, 16–23, 27–28
     fiscal policy 22
     intervention 16–17, 22–23
     monetary policy 23
     subsidies 16–17
     supply-side policy 22
     taxes 16, 20, 22
gross domestic product 19

income inequality 21
inflation 21

jobs 6, 20, 27

law of demand 8–9, 16
law of supply 10–11

macroeconomics 18–19, 22
market system 12–15
microeconomics 12–13
modelling, economic 7
monopolies 27

pollution 15–17, 28
price, importance of 7–10
producers 7, 10–15

rates, interest 23
resources 4–6, 13–19, 24, 28
        renewable resources 28

self-interest 7–9, 12–13, 15
standard of living 20, 25, 27
suppliers 7, 10–15, 18
supply and demand 8–19, 27
       equilibrium 13, 15, 19

trade, international 24–27

unemployment 20, 27